595

D0847754

GOD A PRESENT HELP

H. Emilie Cady

Unity Books
Unity Village, Missouri 64065

Revised Edition—1985

Cover design by
Judy Gehrlein

Cover photo by
Keith McKinney

Contents

UNITY IS A link in the great educational movement inaugurated by Jesus Christ; our objective is to discern the truth in Christianity and prove it. The truth that we teach is not new, neither do we claim special revelations or discovery of new religious principles. Our purpose is to help and teach mankind to use and prove the eternal Truth taught by the Master.—*Charles Fillmore, cofounder of Unity.*

I

Good Tidings of Great Joy

*"Come to me, all who labor and are heavy
laden, and I will give you rest."*
(Matt. 11:28)

Suppose some dear, lifelong friend in whose
ability, resources, and faithfulness you have the
utmost confidence should come to you today and
say: "Friend, rejoice; I have brought you some
good news, almost too good to seem true, but
true nevertheless. From this day all things in your
life may be changed. You have inherited a large
fortune. In fact I have come to bring it to you,
together with a message of love and goodwill.
Everything that money can buy is now yours for
the taking."

What do you think would be the effect of such
news upon you?

At first the glad tidings might seem too good to believe; but if this friend reiterated his statement, giving not only verbal assurances but tangible evidence of its truth, do you think you would hesitate, and question, and quibble about taking the proffered gift? I think not. Instead your heart would leap within you with great and inexpressible joy as you began to realize all that this good news meant, if true. It would mean relief from pressing care, cessation of the gnawing anxiety about making ends meet, ability to gratify your lifelong craving for the beautiful in art and literature, time to read, think, travel, live; and above all else, it would mean the ability to help hundreds of others who are struggling with the problems of sickness, poverty, and discouragement.

Then suppose that before you had mentally quite taken in the new situation this messenger of good news should say: "Friend, in addition to this I have found a physician who has never failed to cure every kind of bodily disease from which you are suffering, and if you will come with me to him, he assures me that he can cure you." How long would a person stand undecided about accepting these two gifts? How long would anyone hesitate while he argued with the messenger about his doubts and fears, his unworthiness, or his lack of ability to use these gifts properly?

Yet this is exactly what we as Christians do with God our Father. A messenger has been sent with a definite, positive message: *". . . good news of a great joy which will come to all the people."* (Luke 2:10) The good news is this: *". . . the kingdom of heaven is at hand,"* (Matt. 3:2) here, now. We have read and heard the story since childhood, with varying emotions. At first with a child's understanding and simple trust we imagined that it meant just what it said. But as we went on in the Christian life we found ourselves losing the child's idea and coming to believe that the message does not mean at all what it says. The very simplicity of it made our older, wiser minds recoil from taking it as it reads, and this in spite of the truth uttered by Jesus: *". . . unless you turn and become like children you will never enter the kingdom of heaven."* (Matt. 18:3)

Jesus' first sermon of which we have any record was preached in Nazareth.

And he came to Nazareth, where he had been brought up; and he went to the synagogue, as his custom was, on the sabbath day. And he stood up to read; and there was

3

*given to him the book of the prophet Isaiah.
He opened the book and found the place
where it was written,*

*"The Spirit of the Lord is upon me, because
he has anointed me to preach good news to
the poor. He has sent me to proclaim release
to the captives and recovering of sight to the
blind, to set at liberty those who are oppressed, to proclaim the acceptable year of
the Lord."*

*And he closed the book, and gave it back to
the attendant, and sat down; and the eyes of
all in the synagogue were fixed on him. And
he began to say to them, "Today this scrip-
ture has been fulfilled in your hearing."*
(Luke 4:16-21)

In other words, the Lord God hath sent Me,
Jesus Christ, and I am now this day here present
with you *to comfort all who mourn,* to deliver
the captives from prison, to give sight to the
blind, to heal the sick, *to give them a garland instead of ashes, the oil of gladness instead of
mourning, the mantle of praise instead of a faint
spirit.* (Isa. 61:2, 3) This is the good news I have
come to bring to you from God your Father.

As time went on Jesus sent out twelve men
whom He chose to spread this good news, giving

to each the same power and the same commission, that is, the power to heal the sick, to cast out devils, and so forth, and to preach this practical gospel:

"And preach as you go, saying, 'The kingdom of heaven is at hand.' Heal the sick, raise the dead, cleanse lepers, cast out demons." (Matt. 10:7, 8)

When John the Baptist sent two of his disciples to ask Jesus if He really was the Christ or if they should look for another, He said, as evidence that He really was the messenger sent from God:

"Go and tell John what you hear and see: the blind receive their sight and the lame walk, lepers are cleansed and the deaf hear, and the dead are raised up, and the poor have good news preached to them." (Matt. 11:4, 5)

After Jesus had risen and as He was about to part from His disciples He told them that their future mission in this world was to be exactly what He had been: *"As the Father has sent me, even so I send you."* (John 20:21)

In other words, as the Father sent Him to preach the good news that the kingdom of heaven is here now, that the sick can be healed now, that the blind can receive sight at once, that the brokenhearted can be made to rejoice, that all this spirit of mourning and sorrow and heaviness can be changed into joy and praise, so send I you into the world to preach the same glad tidings to them that sit in darkness and discouragement to tell all people that God is their Savior, their genuine right-at-hand-this-moment deliverance.

As Jesus continued in the ministry of such a gospel, His heart was wrought upon as He saw how ignorant the people were of the real truth of God's desire toward them, and we read:

> *After this the Lord appointed seventy others, and sent them on ahead of him, two by two, into every town and place where he himself was about to come. And he said to them . . . "heal the sick . . . and say to them, 'The kingdom of God has come near to you.' "*
>
> *The seventy returned with joy, saying, "Lord, even the demons are subject to us in your name!" And he said to them ". . . Behold, I have given you authority to tread upon serpents and scorpions, and over all the power of the enemy; and nothing shall hurt you. Nevertheless do not rejoice in this, that the spirits are subject to you; but rejoice that your names are written in heaven."*
> (Luke 10:1, 2, 9, 17-30)

In other words, rejoice not so much because you are able to make these marvelous demonstrations of power as because your spiritual eyes have been opened to the real relations between God your Father and yourself.

Jesus Christ did many marvelous works in the material world; and in thus appointing others to help Him in His work among men—in increasing members as the work enlarged—and giving to them the power to manifest the same mastery over untoward material conditions, He showed conclusively that at least part of the gospel deals directly with God's deliverance of His children from sickness, poverty, and all manner of human suffering. The early Christians for three hundred years following the resurrection of Jesus believed this and did the mighty works that He said should be done in His name. Then they lapsed into worldliness and the power was lost.

Every Christian recognizes today that the work of Jesus in the world was to establish a kingdom of righteousness, peace, and love; to teach us a higher law than the one we had known, that of "an eye for an eye, and a tooth for a tooth." But many entirely overlook the fact that in addition to teaching us a higher way of living, Jesus proved to us by daily ministering among the sorrowing and sick, and by giving the same power

7

and commission to those whom He sent out to continue the work in His name and stead, that God is in His world to do both; that is, to help His children live a better life, and also to be to them life, health, comfort, all material things needed.

There is no record that Jesus ever said to the sick who came to Him that continued suffering would develop in them greater spiritual virtues. He did not say to the leper: "Your disease is the result of sensuality. I will not heal you, because if I do you will continue in the same way of sin." He only said: *"Do you want to be healed?"* . . . *"Rise, take up your pallet, and walk."* (John 5:6, 8)

He did not say to anyone who came for healing or for any other deliverance, "Yes, I will heal you, but the healing will not become manifest for several months—just to test your faith." Nor did He say to anyone who came, "I heal many; but it is not God's will for you to be healed, and you must be submissive to His will." Oh, the deadening effect of this kind of submission! Who but knows it!

He did not let the people go hungry, saying it was their own carelessness not to have provided bread and they must not expect a miracle to be wrought to encourage such carelessness. He first fed them with spiritual food, to be sure; but immediately following that He ministered with equal ease and alacrity to their physical hunger, even though the lack may have been their own fault. When the widow of Nain, with heartbreak such as only a mother can know, followed the bier upon which lay dead her soul's pride, her beautiful and only son, Jesus did not simply comfort her with platitudes or even by bringing some superhuman joy in the place of sorrow. She wanted her boy back; and He gave her what she wanted.

Peter lacked money for the tax gatherer. Did Jesus say: "Peter, the gift of God is spiritual riches. Do not ask for worldly money, for God has nothing to do with that. If you have no money for taxes be patient and work it out some way"; and then did He leave Peter to anxiety and care? Not at all. He instantly supplied the thing that was needed.

Jesus Christ came to show us the Father, to reveal to us the will of the Father toward us. Did He not say: *"He who has seen me has seen the Father . . . The words that I say to you I do not speak on my own authority; but the Father who dwells in me does his works"?* (John 14:9, 10) Then how can we in our minds separate God from His world as we do? Most of us confine

Him to His spiritual kingdom alone. We know that He wants to give us purity and spiritual grace. Every Christian believes this. But do we know or believe that He wants us to have the other desires of our heart as well? Do we believe He wants to heal our bodies, provide our taxes, feed our hunger? Do we believe that Jesus Christ really is *the same yesterday and today and for ever?* Do we believe that *he is not God of the dead, but of the living;* that the kingdom of heaven is here at hand this moment, only that our eyes are so held by sense conditions we do not see it?

He said: *". . . You will know the truth, and the truth will make you free."* (John 8:32) Then if we are not free we do not yet know the Truth but are believing in a lie, or in the lack of Truth at least. Is this not so?

Is dumb, hopeless submission to suffering a spiritual grace? I do not believe it is. Jesus never taught that it is. He taught us nonresistance to evil; that is, not to fight evil as an entity. But He also taught us how to obtain absolute victory over and deliverance from evil of whatever form by coming into living and vital touch with Christ. This He declared to be God's will toward us; and He demonstrated it continually by delivering all who were bound in any manner by sin, sickness, suffering, or sorrow.

An earnest Christian mother related to me a few years ago a story of her little boy, who had the whooping cough. The mother had taught the boy to pray; and whenever he felt one of the dreaded coughing spells approaching he instantly ran and fell on his knees, exclaiming, "Oh, Mamma, let me pray, let me pray quickly so God will keep this cough away!" The mother told of the difficulty she had had in explaining to the child that while it was good to pray, yet he must not expect God to stop the cough, because when one has the whooping cough it is natural to cough! Now, according to Jesus' teachings and His dealings with people here on Earth, is this not just what the boy might and ought to have expected God to do? *". . . Unless you turn and become like children, you will never enter the kingdom of heaven."* (Matt. 18:3)

> *. . . Call upon me in the day of trouble;*
> *I will deliver you . . . .* (Psalms 50:15)

This is the gospel, the *"good news of a great joy which will come to all the people."* This is something of what He meant when He said: *" 'The kingdom of heaven is at hand.' "* Surely He meant more than we can ask or think when He said: *"Come to me."*

11

II

The Will of God

"What father among you, if his son asks for a fish, will instead of a fish give him a serpent; or if he asks for an egg, will give him a scorpion? If you then, who are evil, know how to give good gifts to your children, how much more will the heavenly Father give the Holy Spirit to those who ask him!" (Luke 11:11-13)

God's will for us is not sorrow, poverty, loneliness, death, and all the other forms of suffering that we usually associate with the expression, "Thy will be done."

Paul said: *For in him all the fulness of God was pleased to dwell . . . .* (Col. 1:19) This means fullness of love, fullness of life, fullness of power, fullness of joy, fullness of all good; and

Christ abideth in you. . . . *The fulness of him who fills all in all.* (Eph. 1:23)

God is not death; He is life. God is not hate and sorrow; He is love and joy. God is not weakness and failure; He is power and success.

When Jesus Christ was here on Earth He said He came to represent the Father, that is, to be to us as the Father would be; to do to us and for us what the Father would do: *"He who has seen me has seen the Father . . . ."* (John 14:9) *"Truly, truly, I say to you, the Son can do nothing of his own accord, but only what he sees the Father doing; for whatever he does, that the Son does likewise."* (John 5:19) Jesus never gave sorrow or sickness to anyone. Did He not say, *"These things I have spoken to you, that my joy may be in you, and that your joy may be full"?* (John 15:11) Did He not definitely say, *". . . I came that they may have life, and have it abundantly"?* (John 10:10)

It has been urged by many good people that Jesus meant only spiritual life. Well, He did not say so, and *the common people* who *heard him gladly* were not desiring or seeking spiritual life. They wanted at that time health for their sick ones; and in that day life meant just what the common people would understand today by life. Oh, how the human intellect in its ignorance and egotism has twisted and turned and distorted the plain, simple words of the Master in order to make them conform to its darkened understanding!

Truly the . . . *light shines in the darkness, and the darkness has not overcome it.* (John 1:5)

"Jesus must have meant so and so, because we do not see how He could have meant otherwise," says the intellect of man. What a pity that we should have grown so far away from the very simplicity of the *". . . good news of a great joy which will come to all the people. . . ."* (Luke 2:10)

Truly, *the unspiritual man does not receive the gifts of the Spirit of God, for they are folly to him, and he is not able to understand them because they are spiritually discerned.* (I Cor. 2:14)

Jesus gave physical health for physical sickness, and cured people. He gave life where there had been physical death, as to the daughter of Jairus; He gave power and courage to the disciples where weakness and fear had existed, so that the once cowardly Peter became a very rock of courage and strength forever after; He gave joy for sorrow, as when He restored to Mary and Martha the brother who had left them.

All of the conditions from which the human heart shrinks He changed for the mere asking.

He did not have to be begged and besought for weeks and months. He changed the conditions. How? Not by merely giving the suffering one a spirit of submission, which is but another word for a state of absolute benumbment and discouragement, but by removing the cause of the sorrow and restoring life, joy, power; by giving back something to fill to fullness the very gap that existed. *"If you then, who are evil, know how to give good gifts to your children, how much more will the heavenly Father give the Holy Spirit to those who ask him!"* (Luke 11:13) *Every good endowment and every perfect gift is from above, coming down from the Father of lights with whom there is no variation or shadow due to change.* (James 1:17)

Throughout all the ages of the biblical record it was the experience and teaching of prophets, priests, and kings unto God that more of God in one's life meant more of good.

Life is good, and we all desire more of it. *"I am . . . the life,"* (John 11:25) said Jesus Christ. *"I came that they may have life, and have it abundantly,"* (John 10:10) more life because of His indwelling.

"These things have I spoken to you, that my joy may be in you, and that your joy may be full." (John 15:11) There is fullness of joy

because of His joy in us.

"Peace I leave with you; my peace I give to you; not as the world gives do I give to you." (John 14:27) *". . . the peace of God, which passes all understanding . . . ."* (Phil. 4:7) The peace of God alone is able to keep our hearts and minds overflowing with joy.

". . . You shall receive power when the Holy Spirit has come upon you" (Acts 1:8); that is, after more of the Spirit of God comes into your life. Greater power is only more of God, of All-Power.

"Behold, my servants shall eat . . . behold, my servants shall drink . . . behold, my servants shall rejoice . . . behold, my servants shall sing for gladness of heart . . . . They shall build houses and inhabit them." (Isa. 65:13, 14, 21)

The Christ, the Son of God, speaking through Jesus of Nazareth, in His prayer of thanksgiving to our Father said: *". . . as thou, Father, art in me, and I in thee, that they also may be in us . . . . I in them and thou in me, that they may become perfectly one . . . ."* (John 17:21, 23)

Marvelous way, is it not, in which the creature is to be made perfect and known and loved and great: simply letting God's will be done in us and in our circumstances and surroundings? Yet heretofore one's saying, "Thy will be done," has been associated in mind only with death and suffering and failure, and with a forced submission to these un-Godlike conditions, as though God were the author of them. . . . *God is not a God of confusion but of peace.* (I Cor. 14:33) Oh, how in our ignorance we have mistaken and misunderstood God, in consequence of which we are today pygmies when He wanted to make us giants in love and health and power by manifesting more of Himself through us! We would not let Him, because we have been afraid to say, "Have your way with me; be in me as you will."

If then it is God's will to give us all these good gifts, how is it that as good and sincere Christians, really and truly God's children, we so often lack them all and cry in vain for help? It is because we have not known how to deal with the things that are contrary to His will, and how to take that which God has freely given.

How are we to deal with the things that we know are contrary to the Father's will as it was revealed by Jesus Christ?

Take sickness, for instance. We are to remember that Jesus repeatedly spoke of it as not of God but rather of Satan. An instance is the case of the *woman who had had a spirit of infirmity for eighteen years; she was bent over and could not fully straighten herself.* (Luke 13:11) Of her

He said: *". . . ought not this woman, a daughter of Abraham whom Satan bound for eighteen years, be loosed from this bond on the sabbath day?"* (Luke 13:16)

On another occasion . . . *a blind and dumb demoniac was brought to him, and he healed him, so that the dumb man spoke and saw.* (Matt. 12:22) When the Pharisees, who knew Jesus as a son of David, saw this and accused Him of working by the power of Beelzebul, the prince of devils, He said: *". . . if Satan casts out Satan, he is divided against himself; how then will his kingdom stand? . . . But if it is by the Spirit of God that I cast out demons, then the kingdom of God has come upon you."* (Matt. 12:26, 28)

Let us then recognize, as Jesus did, that according to the will of God we ought to be loosed from our infirmities. Let us meet the issue fairly and squarely without a moment's fear or hesitation, acting in His name and by His authority. *"And these signs will accompany those who believe: in my name they will cast out demons."* (Mark 16:17) Let us boldly say: "Get you behind me Satan! You are a lie and the father of all lies. Sickness is not of God, and I will not submit to it. God is life. He is almighty, and His will is to manifest life more abundant through me. Christ does and shall reign in this body. His will is done." This is the attitude we must take.

How are we to deal with our Father's will? Exactly as with any other will.

What should we do if some friend left a will giving something very desirable to us? We should first make sure by probate that it was his will; then we should not leave a stone unturned in having it executed. If we met with some opposition and delay we should push the harder and with more determination to obtain that which by right of inheritance belonged to us.

Shouldn't we do the same regarding the will of God our Father? This will was made ages ago, giving to whoever will ask and pray for it. This is the only limitation He has placed on any human being: *". . . whatever you ask in prayer, you will receive, if you have faith."* (Matt. 21:22) *". . . If you ask anything in my name, I will do it."* (John 14:14) *". . . Put me to the test . . . if I will not open the windows of heaven for you and pour down for you an overflowing blessing."* (Mal. 3:10)

God has already done His part in full. In Judges 18:10 it is written: *". . . God has given it into your hands, a place where there is no lack of anything that is in the earth;"* that is, of anything the human heart desires. Jesus said,

". . . you will receive, if you have faith." (Matt. 21:22) Whatever you desire is yours by right of inheritance because you are His child, and children are the natural and rightful heirs to all that the Father has. In the redemption wrought out by Christ we have become . . . *heirs of God and fellow heirs with Christ* . . . . (Rom. 8:17) We are all sons and daughters of God, through faith in Jesus Christ. He has thus assured us that all things are ours by right, and:

God is not man, that he should lie,
or a son of man, that he should repent.
Has he said, and will he not do it?
Or has he spoken, and will he not fulfil it?
(Num. 23:19)

Now it only remains for us to prove the will by affirmation and trust; to prove Him and see if He will not do all that He has promised. The Holy Spirit alone is the executor of God's will, but even this executor can do nothing for us unless we take the right attitude.

"Arise," He says, *". . . Do not be slow to go, and enter in and possess the land."* (Judg. 18:9) Thus there is something definite for us to do. In proving God there must be no meek submission to the things coming upon us that we know are

contrary to His will for us, as that will was revealed by Jesus Christ.

Did Jesus ever tell anyone that it was God's will for him to suffer lack, or be sick, or be a failure in any way? If any such vision of God's will is in your mind, rise up instantly, and in the name of Christ put it forever out of your thoughts as unworthy of a loving Father, and doubly unworthy of yourself, His offspring. When any of these things come upon you, arise at once and claim your rightful inheritance. *". . . I am your portion and your inheritance . . ."* saith the Lord. (Num. 18:20) He is life, wisdom, peace, joy, strength, power. Remember that He has given it into your hands, although to you it may not yet be visible: a place where there is no want of anything.

When God said to Moses, "I AM," it was as though He said: "I am this moment to you anything that you have the courage to claim, but you must prove Me. I am the supply of every lack in your life, but you must take it, and then stand still and see the salvation that I will work for you."

To us in our spiritual impotence Jesus says today, as He did to the infirm man at the Pool of Bethzatha, *"Do you want to be healed?"* (John 5:6) That is, "Do you will it, and not simply languidly desire it? Are you determined to have that executed which you are satisfied is God's will for you? Well, then I will it too,'' and it is done.

Listen! ''If thou wilt'' brings no visible answer to prayer. But a definite, positive will-not-be-put-off attitude, a determined ''I will have your will done in this matter'' is a force that always brings results into manifestation.

III

Life More Abundant

"I came that they may have life, and have it abundantly." (John 10:10)

All life is the breath of God. When God created man He . . . *breathed into his nostrils the breath of life; and man became a living being.* (Gen. 2:7)

Life then, that mysterious something which man has tried in vain to analyze, to weigh, and to measure, even to produce; life, I say, is the breath of God. *"The spirit of God has made me, and the breath of the Almighty gives me life."* (Job 33:4) Is it any wonder that man tries in vain to catch this life principle, to harness it, to produce it?

There is but one kind of life in the universe. All life is divine; all life is the breath of God. All life is God made manifest, and the manifestation varies according to the degree, so to speak, in which God, the breath of life, comes forth into visibility through the various forms, *according to the measure of Christ's gift.* In the rock an invisible something holds the atoms from flying off from one another, as would be their natural bent. Natural science calls this the force of cohesion. Cohesive force is but another name for the breath of God prevading the atoms of the rocks. Life in the vegetable, the grass, the tree is all one and the same life manifested in larger measure than in the rock. Man is the fullest, highest form of God manifested as life.

We read that *in the beginning* this mysterious something, which we cannot see, feel, or handle but which is plainly stated to be the ''breath of God,'' was breathed into man and *man became a living being.* Has the manner of creation changed any since the ''first beginning''? Is it not the beginning for every new creation today? Is not the life of every being the very breath of God today just as much as it ever was? Are not we all equally His children, His offspring by inheritance? Yea, verily.

God's breath is what God is; that is, it is of the same nature and substance. If God is life, His breath is life. If God's breath is our life that life must be like God, eternal in every child He creates. Without that breath of God given individually none of us could exist today. Neither the soul of man nor the body of man has life in itself. Both are made alive and kept alive momently by the Spirit that is God pervading and permeating them. . . . *The Spirit gives life.* (II Cor. 3:6) *For you have died, and your life is hid with Christ in God.* (Col. 3:3)

Jesus came that we might have life and that we might *have it abundantly.* He came to show us our true relation to the source of all life, and to teach us how to draw consciously upon God our Father for more abundant life as we need it. This does not mean spiritual life alone but life for the entire being. Is our heart cold, and is our love dead? We cannot analyze love, we cannot work it up at will; but we know that God is love and love is God. What we need is more of God, love, breathed into our hearts until we are transformed into new creatures by divine love. . . . *He breathed on them, and said to them, "Receive the Holy Spirit."* (John 20:22) Something was given by His breathing on them.

Do we lack wisdom? It is not more laborious study that we need in order to obtain it, but a fresh supply of Omniscience—all-knowledge, all-wisdom—breathed into this intellect by Him who

. . . gives to all men generously and without reproaching . . . . (James 1:5) It is more of the breath of the living God we need.

If we are weak and unstable in character, if we are failures mentally, spiritually, or physically, if we feel ourselves in any way bound or limited, it is because we need more of this mysterious breath of God, which is power, life, freedom. *"He is not God of the dead, but of the living."* (Matt. 22:32)

Health is more life. Drugs will not give life. Travel and change of scene, so often resorted to in illness of mind and body, will not give life except insofar as they tend to relax the tense, rigid mind and body and permit God—who is always in process of outgoing as life toward us His children—to flow in to fill the lack. We do not have to beseech God. Life more abundant rushes into the souls and bodies of men, as air does into a vacuum, the moment they learn how consciously to relax and, turning toward God, let it.

People who are persistently ill or unsuccessful in any way say they are tired of it all and want to die. They know not what they say. They do not understand. It is not death they want but more life. This breath of the Almighty is to us the only health and strength, the only power and success of either mind or body. *. . . With thee is the* *fountain of life.* (Psalms 36:9) . . . *He who finds me finds life . . . .* (Prov. 8:35) *In him* [Christ, this very Christ who now lives within each of us] *was life, and the life was the light of men.* (John 1:4) *If the Spirit of him who raised Jesus from the dead dwells in you, he who raised Christ Jesus from the dead will give life to your mortal bodies also through his Spirit which dwells in you.* (Rom. 8:11)

Life is God's gift. The outer life is but the out-flowing of the inner life; and that inner life is momentarily fed from the fountain of life through Christ at the center of our being. God gives His own life freely to all who can receive it.

If this be true, that the breath of the Almighty is the only health of mind or body, why look else-where?

What then are we to do?

Change our minds. Turn around. If through ignorance of the only and unfailing source of all life we have turned our backs upon God and our faces toward human helps, like drugs, change of environment, and the like, let us halt, face about!

He came to his own home, and his own people received him not. (John 1:11) *"I am the resurrection and the life,"* (John 11:25) says Christ within you today. Notice that it is "I am," not

27

"I will be," present tense, not future. "*. . . He who believes in me, though he die, yet shall he live.*" (John 11:25) It is as though He said, "He that believeth on me as the source of his life and turns away from human ways to me as the way, even if he seems to be at the very last gasp of his soul, body, or circumstances, I say he shall be made alive by the same power that was able to raise up Jesus from the dead."

God's gifts are alike to all; but we have to learn how to receive freely that which He gives, how to open ourselves to the inflow of divine life through the Christ at the center of our being, exactly as we would open ourselves to the warm rays of the sun. *But to all who received him, who believed in his name, he gave power to become children of God.* (John 1:12)

Elsewhere we have said that all conscious taking or receiving from God is a mental process. The human mind believes itself, in the matter of life, cut off from God, a separate being, something apart from God. This belief is not correct. The wire of communication between the Creator and His creations is never cut, the channel of inflowing divine life never closed. Each blade of grass receives its life, its springtime renewing force, as directly from the fountain of all life as though it were the only thing in the universe.

How can man by mental process stimulate and increase this inflow of divine life? How can even the least of us consciously draw upon the inexhaustible Fountain for the life more abundant that we need for soul, body, and circumstances?

". . . The words that I have spoken to you are spirit and life," (John 6:63) said the Master. Words. Is there any power or life in words? Let us see. *". . . But only say the word, and my servant will be healed,"* (Matt. 8:8) said the centurion. That was all that was done; but a little farther we read: . . . *the servant was healed at that very moment.* (Matt. 8:13)

". . . So shall my word be that goes forth from my mouth; it shall not return to me empty, but it shall accomplish that which I purpose . . . ." (Isa. 55:11)

All words of Truth are alive with an invisible energy that has power to work miracles. Truth is mighty to accomplish results, but in order to do so it must be spoken into activity. It must be put into words. The same Christ who said, "I am the life," said also, "I am the truth." Life, Truth, Christ are one. The words of Truth that you and I speak in the name and spirit of the Master become His words, full of life and health. Such words set into motion the invisible energy that accomplishes results, and nothing is accomplished when it is quiescent.

Speaking definite, positive words of assurance to oneself or to another has marvelous power to lift and transform, power to fill the fearful, trembling heart and the suffering body with a consciousness of the real living presence of God. There is wondrous life-giving power in definitely and vigorously compelling oneself to *sing to the Lord a new song,* even making it a song of praise and thanksgiving for benefits. Everyone has power through his will, apart from any feeling if need be, to follow the prophet's advice: *Take with you words and return to the Lord.* (Hos. 14:2) No matter how deep or poignant his misery, a person can compel himself by mere willpower to look up to God and say:

> *Bless the Lord, O my soul,*
> *and forget not all his benefits,*
> *who forgives all your iniquity,*
> *who heals all your diseases,*
> *who redeems your life from the Pit,*
> *who crowns you with steadfast love and*
> *mercy,*
> *who satisfies you with good as long as you*
> *live . . . .* (Psalms 103:2-5)

No matter whether you feel like it or not, say

it. Put it into words. Out of the depths of misery begin sincerely and earnestly to speak words of praise and thanksgiving, and soon you will find yourself involuntarily saying:

I fear no evil; for thou art with me . . . my cup overflows. (Psalms 23:4-5)

This is God's way of working to deliver us out of our troubles. Thus He comforts us and gives newness of life through our first "speaking comfortably" to ourselves and to Him the words of Truth. Such words have power to free the channel between our own centers of life and the fountain of all life—channels that may have become clogged by our selfishness or ignorance—so that a great, surging influx of new life can take place. . . . *You shall call your walls Salvation, and your gates Praise.* (Isa. 60:18) Praise and thanksgiving open wide the gates to salvation.

You may say, "What good is this except to uplift my thought, making it easier for me to bear my trouble, illness, sorrow? It cannot change the real, visible conditions." Yes, it can and does. Lazarus was as dead as he ever could be and there was no faintest stirring of life when Jesus lifted up His eyes and said: *"I thank thee, Father . . ."* (Matt. 11:25) Jesus understood that the gates in the wall of salvation from this death would fly wide open at the paean of praise. Every instant that our hearts are thus uplifted in the spirit of gratitude (which, remember, is aroused by our first beginning to speak *words* of gratitude for benefits received) this mighty energy that we have spoken of and that is none other or less than the Spirit of the living God, is working to change, restore, and heal the very trouble that seems about to destroy us.

Oh, how many times this has been proved by those of God's children who, in some degree at least, have come to know the way of the Father's working even as Jesus knew it. How many times they have proven that the solution of the problem, the healing of the illness, depended not upon human effort but entirely upon taking the thought altogether off the distress and centering it, by main force of will if need be, upon thanking and blessing God for all His benefits. The work accomplished is not necessarily by might or power, but by Spirit. This is a spiritual law, infallible and unchangeable, a law that works; and many times it is the only thing that does work.

No one is so weak in will but that he can thus compel himself to *"take words, and speak to God,"* even as he would take hold of a mighty

32

lever to lift a heavy weight.

And let him who is thirsty come . . . . (Rev. 22:17)

IV

Christ in You

Though Christ a thousand times in
Bethlehem be born,
If He's not born in thee, thy soul is all
forlorn.
—Johann Scheffler

Man is a threefold being composed of spirit, soul, and body so intermingled, so blended into one that it is beyond the finite mind to say where one ends and the other begins. We read that when man was created he was made in the image and likeness of God. No intelligent person can make the mistake of supposing that God has parts like the human body or that the external man is in any way the image and likeness of God.

God is Spirit, God is life, God is love and wisdom and power. God is all good. Can anyone tell me the active principles composing life? Can anyone analyze love for me? Can anyone weigh or measure wisdom? Can anyone catch and box up, see, or handle Spirit? Nay, verily. God is Spirit; and the real man made in His image is Spirit also. Spirit is substance. Substance (from Latin *sub,* under, and *stare,* to stand) is that invisible, intangible but real something which as its indestructible core and cause stands under, or at the center of, every visible thing.

That there is but one substance of which all things visible and invisible are made is conceded by all scientists, whether spiritual or material. This one substance is Spirit, forever invisible but indestructible. . . . *The world was created by the word of God, so that what is seen was made out of things which do not appear.* (Heb. 11:3) God is not only the creative cause of every visible form of intelligence or life at its beginning, but at each moment of its existence. He lives within every created thing at its very center as the life, the ever-renewing, recreating, upbuilding cause of it. This is not pantheism, which declares that the visible universe, taken or conceived of as a whole, is God. No, far from it. God expresses Himself in visible ways. Man is His fullest, most complete expression. God is the living, warm, throbbing life that pervades our being. He is the quickening intelligence that keeps our minds balanced and steady throughout all the vicissitudes of life. He never is and never can be for a moment separated from His creation. *Do you not know that you are God's temple and that God's Spirit dwells in you?* (I Cor. 3:16) *The King of Israel, the Lord, is in your midst;* (Zeph. 3:15) not in the midst of the community at large but in the midst of you individually.

God is the Father of our spirit, of our real self. We are His offspring, His children. *There is one body and one Spirit . . . one God and Father of us all, who is above all and through all and in all.* (Eph. 4:4, 6) God has made all His children alike. He has no favorites. The spirit of man always has been and always will be in His image while creation continues, no matter what the external man does to hide that image. More than once Jesus gave public recognition to the fact of our oneness with Himself as sons of God—even as He is the Son—and joint heirs with Him. *". . . Go to my brethren and say to them, I am ascending to my Father and your Father, to my God and your God,"* said He to Mary. (John 20:17)

The moment we recognize God as the Father of the spirits of men, and therefore the Father of all men, that moment we recognize a new and vital relationship of all men to one another, we say "our Father" with new depth and meaning. That moment we step out forever from all narrow, selfish loves, all "me and mine," into the broad universal love that encompasses the whole world and we recognize our oneness with all.

We are made in the image of God. Then is this eating, drinking, sensuous creature we see the image of God? Not at all. But the divine spark at the center of our being, the ever-renewed breath of God, which is the life, the intelligence, of this person, be it full or limited, is God's image, is part of God Himself. Is the ugly, rough piece of marble, with only a nose or a mouth visible, a statue? No, but it will be when the sculptor has finished with it. The perfect statue is there, but hidden, awaiting the touch of the master's hand to bring it forth.

Jesus primarily taught men how to live, to repent of their sins, to turn from all wrongdoing, to love others even to the laying down of their lives for their enemies if necessary. Toward the last of His ministry He said: *"I have yet many things to say to you, but you cannot bear them now. When the Spirit of truth comes, he will guide you into all the truth; for he will not speak on his own authority, but whatever he hears he will speak, and he will declare to you the things that are to come."* (John 16:12-13) Jesus had been to them a visible savior. He had shown them that He had power on Earth to forgive sin, to heal the sick, and raise the dead. He had called Himself the life, the door, the way. But after it all He said He had not told them all He knew as yet; they could not bear it then. *"And I will pray the Father, and he will give you another Counselor, to be with you for ever . . . for he dwells with you, and will be in you."* (John 14:16-17)

Thus Jesus recognized that a personal savior to whom people could go, outside of themselves, was not enough; such a scheme of salvation had its limitations. There must be an inner spiritual birth to each one, a consciousness of an indwelling Christ ever-present within him to be his guide and teacher when He, Jesus, was no longer visible. *"I will not leave you desolate,"* He said to His disciples, *"I will come to you. . . . In that day you will know that I am in my Father, and you in me, and I in you."* (John 14:18-20) In all of Paul's early teaching he spoke only of the Son of man, Jesus, who had been crucified and was risen. But in later years, as he grew in grace and in the knowledge of Truth, he spoke to his spiritual children: *. . . I am again in travail until Christ be formed in you!* (Gal. 4:19) He also spoke of *the mystery hidden for ages and genera-*

tions but now made manifest to his saints. . . .
which is Christ in you, the hope of glory. (Col.
1:26, 27)

What did Jesus mean? What did Paul mean?
Is there then a higher, fuller birth than the one
that many Christians know, that of following
after the crucified Jesus, the son of Mary, who is
and ever must be a personality outside ourselves?

Surely there is. It is not easy to explain the
relation that Jesus, the Man of Galilee, bears to
the Christ of God who is to be formed in us;
scarcely possible by words to explain the mystery
. . . *which is Christ in you, the hope of glory.* It
cannot be put into words. It comes to one as a
revelation; and, thus coming, is as real as one's
very existence. It was not the man Jesus, the personality, the Son of man that was to be the
Savior, for that part of Jesus was human. He
spoke of it as such, saying that of His mortal
self, He could do nothing, that the Father abiding in Him did his works. It was the Christ, the
Anointed, the very divine at the center of His being who came forth and did the works through
Jesus. The Comforter that He promised was to
be the Holy Spirit. The very Spirit of this same
Father who abode in Jesus was to abide within
them and us. This same Spirit, this Christ, to
whom is given all power is formed by a spiritual

birth at the center of your being and mine and abides there. He "who is the image of the invisible God" becomes "the firstborn of all creations"; that is, He is the first coming forth of the invisible Father into the visible creature. He abides within us first as a "babe" (or in small degree); but as He grows and increases in stature in proportion as we recognize Him there, with encouragement and a sort of wooing, so to speak, we make room for the "Babe in the Inn."

There comes to be in this sweet and holy relation a living touch, an intimate sort of intersphering of our whole being with the divine source of all good and all giving. We become conscious of a new relationship between the living, indwelling Christ, unto whom is given all power, and the creature whose needs are unlimited. The very mind of Christ that was in Jesus is in you. The infinite supply for soul, body, and circumstances is at hand in this indwelling Christ, *in whom are hid all the treasures of wisdom and knowledge.* (Col. 2:3) . . . *The fulness of him . . . fills all in all.* (Eph. 1:23) What a marvelous, almost incomprehensible relationship!

How are we, in our entirety, soul and body, to be made perfect? By striving and effort? By lopping off branches of the old tree here and there?

By cutting off this habit and that habit? Not at all. None of these is the way laid down by Christ. He said: *"I am the way . . . ."* (John 14:6) He said: *"I in them and thou in me, that they may become perfectly one . . ."* (John 17:23) We are perfected by His perfect life dwelling within the imperfect life and filling it with His own fullness. We are made perfect, entire, by this I-in-them coming forth into visibility, because of our waiting upon Him in recognition of His indwelling presence and our continued affirmation that He does now manifest Himself as the perfect One through us. *"He must increase, but I must decrease."* (John 3:30)

V

Faith

"Ask, and it will be given you; seek, and you will find; knock, and it will be opened to you. For every one who asks receives, and he who seeks finds, and to him who knocks it will be opened." (Matt. 7:7, 8)

What could Jesus have meant when, speaking as one having authority, He made such a sweeping, and to the poor human mind almost incomprehensible, statement as that quoted above?

We pray, we ask, believing that we are going to receive, but we receive not. Again and again this happens until we grow sick and our courage fails because of our unanswered prayers, and we begin to say, "God does not answer. I don't have sufficient faith or the right kind of faith." Because of repeated failures we are benumbed, and though we still pray we seldom expect an answer. Is not this so?

Where is the trouble?

Many Christians mistake hope for faith. Hope expects an answer sometime in the future; faith takes it as having already been given. Hope looks forward; faith declares that she has received even before there is the slightest visible evidence. Our way is to declare something done after it has become obvious to the senses; God's way is to declare it done before there is anything whatever in sight. This declaring, "It is finished," when there is still no visible evidence has power to bring the desired object into visibility. . . . *The world was created by the word of God* [God's declaring that it was done], *so that what is seen was made out of things which do not appear.* (Heb. 11:3) That is, things that are seen were not made of visible but of invisible substance by the spoken word of God. If we expect anything from God we must conform to His way of working.

Listen to Paul's definition of faith: . . . *faith is the assurance of things hoped for, the conviction of things not seen.* (Heb. 11:1) In other words, faith takes right hold of the invisible substance of the things desired and brings into the world of evidence or visibility the things that before were not seen. There is but one substance from which the real of all things is made. This substance is ever present but invisible. It is all around us and fills the universe as the atmosphere we breathe covers the Earth. In it we live and move and have our being, for it is the divine presence or substance. It is the unseen but real and eternal that always "stands under" and "within" the seen but temporal.

Faith upon which depends all answer to prayer is not, as some people think, a flighty mental condition that it is difficult to catch and hold. If this were so, the child of God might well despair. But there is a faith that might be called understanding faith that is based upon principles as unerring as those of mathematics. It was of this faith that the Man of Galilee spoke when He said: *"All things are possible to him who believes."* (Mark 9:23)

Jesus invariably spoke as one having authority. He had proved that whereof He spoke, and He knew positively. He knew that all God's dealings with man were based upon an immutable law, a law that if complied with is bound from its very nature to work out certain results, no matter who or what manner of man it is that complies with that law. He never went into details as to how or why God's laws work; but positively, in a few concise words, He spoke the law and left the working of it to be proved by ''whosoever will.''

What is this understanding faith upon which the literal fulfillment of all God's promises rests?

''There are some things which God has so indissolubly joined together that it is impossible for even Him to put them asunder. They are bound together by fixed, immutable laws; if we have one of them, we must have the other.''

This may be illustrated by the laws of geometry. For instance, the sum of the interior angles of a triangle is equal to two right angles. No matter how large or small the triangle, no matter where we find it, or who finds it, if we are asked the sum of its angles we can unhesitatingly answer that it is just two right angles. This is absolutely certain. It is certain, even before the triangle is drawn by visible lines; we can know it beforehand, because it is based on unchangeable laws, on the truth or reality of the thing. It was true just as much before anyone recognized it as it is today. Our knowing it or not knowing it does not change the fact. Only in proportion as we come to know it as an eternally true fact can we be benefited by it.

''It is a simple fact that one plus one equals two; it is an eternal truth. You cannot put one and one together without two resulting. You may believe it or not; that does not alter the fact. But unless you do put the one and one together you do not produce the two, for each is eternally dependent on the other.''

The world of spiritual things is governed by law just as unalterable and unfailing as is the law governing the natural world. The so-called supernatural is not beyond law by virtue of being above natural law. It is simply the working of a higher law than any that we, with our limited understanding, have heretofore known; and it is because it operates in a higher realm that we have not understood. When we come into harmony with this higher law we instantly have all the power of God working with us for the very thing we pray for, and we get it. Sometimes a soul comes into this harmony by childlike intuition, and he receives answer to prayer. But we can know the law and put ourselves consciously in harmony with it.

The promises of God are certain, eternal, unchangeable truths that always have been and always must be true, whether in this age or another, whether on the mountaintop or under the sea. A promise, according to Webster's dictionary, gives reason to expect something. It is a declaration that gives to the person to whom it is made the right to expect, to claim, the performance of whatever is promised. God has bound

Himself to His children by promises innumerable, and He has magnified His word above all His name.

For when God made a promise to Abraham, since he had no one greater by whom to swear, he swore by himself . . . . Men indeed swear by a greater than themselves, and in all their disputes an oath is final for confirmation. So when God desired to show more convincingly to the heirs of the promise the unchangeable character of his purpose, he interposed with an oath, so that through two unchangeable things, in which it is impossible that God should prove false, we who have fled for refuge might have strong encouragement to seize the hope set before us. (Heb. 6:13, 16-18)

God is our all-sufficiency in all things. He is the infinite supply, above all that we ask or think, of all that the finite creature can possibly need or desire. The promises are already given. The supply, though unseen by mortal eyes, is at hand.

. . . My God will supply every need of yours according to his riches in glory . . . . (Phil. 4:19) But those who come to God have to believe that God will, indeed, supply those who are in need.

Here are the two fundamental principles on which rests the secret of understanding faith:

First, the supply forever awaits the demand.

Second, the demand must be made before the supply can come forth to fill it.

To recognize these two statements as Truth and affirm them persistently is to comply with the law of God's giving. Faith has nothing to do with visible circumstances. The moment one considers circumstances, one lets go of faith.

When Jesus recognized the unchangeable fact that the supply of every want awaits us just at hand, though unseen, and said: *". . . every one who asks receives . . ."* (Matt. 7:8) He was simply stating a truth as unalterable as that of cause and effect. He knew that there need be no coaxing or pleading, for God has answered before we ask.

". . . Whatever you ask in prayer, believe that you have received it, and it will be yours." (Mark 11:24) *". . . Believe that you have received it . . ."*—present tense! Ah, this is the hard part. Believe that you will (future) receive them. Yes, this is easier. But to say a thing is done when there is no sign of it anywhere—can we do this? Yes, we can, and we must if we would obtain an answer to our prayer. This is the faith on which all receiving depends: "calling that which is not as though it were," simply because God has said so, and holding to it unwaveringly by positive

and continued affirmation that it is done. This is our part of the contract. This is complying with God's law of supply. God said, "I AM," not, "I will be," when He gave His name to Moses. He says, "I AM" to each of us today, and then He leaves us to fill in whatsoever we pray and ask for. I AM health, I AM strength, I AM supply, success, anything we dare take Him for.

How are we to take that which we desire?

Taking is purely a mental process. When Jesus went to the tomb of Lazarus to perform the mighty miracle, He did not plead for help, but He lifted up His eyes and said: *"Father, I thank thee that thou hast heard me. I knew that thou hearest me always . . . ."* (John 11:41, 42) So remembering God's law of supply and demand, we begin to thank Him that He has made Himself our abundant supply and that before we have called He has provided that for which we are about to ask. We continue to thank Him that we do have (not "shall have") the petition desired of Him; and in confidence, but silently and positively, we affirm over and over again that we have it in possession. We must be persistent and unyielding. God said to Joshua: *"Every place that the sole of your foot will tread upon I have given to you . . . ."* (Josh. 1:3) And He says it to us in every act of prayer. Every place that you stand firmly and determinedly upon in affirmation, that have I given you. Dare to claim it; put your foot firmly upon your claim, and you shall have it. Have faith in what you are doing, because you are working with God's own unfailing, unchangeable law, and you cannot fail.

Even in the midst of illness calmly and confidently affirm: *God is in me, my full abundant health now, in spite of this appearance;* for has He not said "I AM"? Jesus said: *"Do not judge by appearances, but judge with right judgment."* (John 7:24) In lack of whatever kind ask and believe that you receive; that is, ask and begin immediately to affirm, even in the absence of any visible evidence, "God is (not will be) my supply right here and now." Be determined about it; He will surely manifest Himself according to His promise.

"Whatsoever you ask in prayer" is the only stipulation governing the relations between us and His I AM. Expecting that anything *will* be given tends to keep it forever in the future, just ahead of the now. Hard though it may be mentally to do it, we must step right over the dividing line and say, "It is done." As far as God's part is concerned, everything has already been given us in Christ. Christ is here present, not far off. Though it is invisible to our mortal eyes, all we

are capable of desiring is here now. All things are in Christ, all are fulfilled in Him now, and He is in you. "In him you are made full." Then can we not say in faith, "All things are mine here and now"?

Persistent, unwavering affirmation that it is done and is made visible now brings into manifestation whatsoever one asks or desires.

VI

Giving and Forgiving

". . . Forgive, if you have anything against any one; so that your Father also who is in heaven may forgive you your trespasses."
(Mark 11:25)

We have become so familiar with the sayings of Jesus that at times they seem to have lost all meaning to us. He said: *"So if you are offering your gift at the altar, and there remember that your brother has something against you, leave your gift there before the altar and go; first be reconciled to your brother, and then come and offer your gift."* (Matt. 5:23, 24) This was equivalent to saying that anyone coming to God in prayer must let go of all ill will toward his brother if he desires or expects any conscious fellowship with God.

If any one says, "I love God," and hates his brother, he is a liar; for he who does not love his brother whom he has seen, cannot love God whom he has not seen. (I John 4:20)

Jesus was speaking in full recognition of the great law governing God's dealings with His children when he said: "*. . . forgive, if you have anything against any one; so that your Father also who is in heaven may forgive you your trespasses.*" We are not for an instant to understand by this that God, in an I-will-give-you-back-as-good-as-you-send spirit, refuses us forgiveness when we do not forgive others. Neither are we to understand that because we fail He is angry with us and turns in an unforgiving mood away from us. Not at all. God is not an overindulgent parent who gives a reward for well-doing and punishes in anger for failing to do well. Such a conception of Him is belittling and unworthy of the thought of any intelligent person.

Let us see if we can find out the law of God's working in this matter of *for*giving as well as in the matter of giving. Our first step is to remember how we are related to God and to our fellow human beings. God is in Christ, and Christ is in us and in all persons. God, the infinite, unfailing source, the great spring and reservoir of All-Good, is forever desirous of outflowing and ever in process of outflowing to His children through Christ. We, God's children, His offspring, are made alive and kept alive by His breath continually renewed in us, and thus in the deepest reality we are never separated from Him for an instant: Him, the life, the love, the mind that is in us, the only power through which we can do anything. If Jesus said, "I can of myself do nothing," how much more must every human being say the same.

Of ourselves, if in reality we are separated from God, we are nothing and can do nothing. But *we have this treasure in earthen vessels, to show that the transcendent power belongs to God and not to us.* (II Cor. 4:7) Christ in us and God in Christ says, *I am . . . the life.* With every breath, we draw in anew this life of God, which is God. And there must be a continual renewal. The breath of yesterday or an hour ago does not suffice for this moment. When we breathe in but little of this breath of life we are only half alive, so to speak. Yet our life is in Christ just the same, waiting for us; and it is not His fault if we take but little of it. No matter how sinful we are or how completely our life is covered and hidden by worldliness or indifference, the source of our life remains unchanged.

So with our inner light, the light of all persons:

wisdom, judgment, knowledge, and so forth. This comes into us momentarily from God through Christ *in whom are hid all the treasures of wisdom and knowledge.* (Col. 2:3) *The true light that enlightens every man was coming into the world.* (John 1:9) To whom was this referring? A few Christians? A few in this church or that church? No, but He is the "true light," lighting every person.

Now if God in Christ is the life of all life, if He is the light of all light, the force of all forces, how is it that some are suffering from lack of life, some are sitting in darkness, some are handicapped by weakness of character and body?

Listen! We are not automatons. We are made in the image and likeness of God, and like Him we have the power of choice, the power of deciding for ourselves: "There is one God, the Father, of whom are all things, and we unto him; and one Lord, Jesus Christ, through whom are all things, and we through him," to be sure. There is but one force, but we each have the power of opening ourselves to this force or closing ourselves to it, whichever we choose. The force lives on whichever we do.

The inner light comes to *"every man . . . coming into the world";* but we may close ourselves to this light either through ignorance or

55

willfulness—the result is the same—and live in darkness. The light within every man goes right on shining just the same, whether he accepts it or rejects it. *The light shines in the darkness, and the darkness has not overcome it.* (John 1:5) In this case the light is shut off through ignorance. *"And this is the judgment, that the light has come into the world, and men loved darkness rather than light, because their deeds were evil. For every one who does evil hates the light, and does not come to the light, lest his deeds should be exposed. But he who does what is true comes to the light, that it may be clearly seen that his deeds have been wrought in God."* (John 3:19-21) Thus is the light voluntarily or willfully shut out, again as a matter of man's choice. Both conditions are dependent on the mental attitude of man. In the first instance he is not conscious that there is light within himself: . . . *the darkness has not overcome it.* In the second instance he stubbornly refuses to come to the light because he "hates the light."

The power that is in us is divine. It is from God, who is omnipotent, but we are given the choice of using or directing this power for either good or evil. The light that is in us is good. It is Christ; but we may elect to use this light for our guidance or for our destruction.

All our relations to God our Father, as we are taught by Jesus, whether we are conscious of it or not, depend on our own mental attitude and not on any changeable attitude of God toward us. From His very nature God is forever in process of giving, just as the sun from its very nature is forever in process of radiating, of shedding abroad, light and heat. The sun does not have to be coaxed and urged to shine. It simply cannot for an instant cease to shine while it remains the sun. The only way we can escape from the direct oncoming of the sun's rays is to interpose something between ourselves and the sun, an act, as you see, that is entirely our own and not that of the sun. Even the sun will continue undisturbed to give forth alike to "the just and the unjust" what it has and is, and let whosoever will take.

So it is with God. He is forever in the process of giving out what He is and has. Nothing can hinder our receiving unless we, consciously or unconsciously, interpose some condition, some mental obstacle between God and ourselves that completely shuts God out.

If we expect to receive anything from God, we must turn our faces toward Him like little children and open our entire being to His incoming. We must not shut Him out by either a tense, rigid, mental condition of anxiety or by an unforgiving spirit. When Jesus said, *". . . forgive . . . so that your Father may forgive your trespasses,"* He understood perfectly that just as we freely direct this divine force toward others, so by our own words and mental attitudes we likewise direct this force toward and through ourselves. In other words, this indwelling Christ is as obedient to us as we are obedient to the Christ.

No one can possibly radiate darkness while he is full of light. *He who says he is in the light and hates his brother is in the darkness still. He who loves his brother abides in the light, and in it there is no cause for stumbling. But he who hates his brother is in the darkness and walks in the darkness, and does not know where he is going, because the darkness has blinded his eyes.* (I John 2:9-11)

The everlasting light abideth in us, but if we shut it off so others cannot receive it, we by the same mental act shut it out of our own consciousness. When we withdraw ourselves from our fellow human beings in any way, particularly when we retain toward anyone an unforgiving spirit (no matter how he may have injured us), we cut off by strangulation, as it were, all the invisible arteries and nerves through which love from God constantly flows into us. It is like ligating an artery between the heart and an extremity. The heart goes right on, but the extremity withers and dies because the source of its nourishment has been cut off.

When by our own acts we thus cut ourselves off from God we become, as someone has said, "a mere bundle of strained nerves, trembling and shaking with fear and weakness and finally dying" because by our own mental attitude we shut off God's life and love, which is ever springing up within us, seeking to flow out through us anew to the world.

We all know what Jesus said to Peter in answer to his question whether one should forgive another seven times: *"I do not say to you seven times, but seventy times seven."* (Matt. 18:22) By this Jesus meant: "Always be in a mental attitude of forgiving, never any other way; and if this is the way God is toward you, how much more should you be so toward your brother." Read the parable on forgiveness that He spoke as it is recorded in Matthew 18:23-35.

Forgiveness demands a mental attitude much more definite than a simple feeling of indifference toward the offending one. To pardon means simply to remit or wipe out the penalty and let the offender go free, but to forgive means much more than this. It means to give "for"; that is, to give positive good in return for the evil received.

59

Is this "a hard saying"? One often hears this phrase: "I can forgive, but I cannot forget." That is not God's way of forgiving. "Their sin will I remember no more" is what He says. Why? Because He keeps right on giving "for," giving us good for our evil.

Nothing else so surely clears out all remembrance of wrongs suffered as definitely and positively as to "give for" the offending one.

If you think you have been wronged by anyone, sit down quietly in your own room and speak out to this person silently. Tell him that you forgive him for the sake of the Christ in him. Tell him that you give him love, love, love in return for anything he may have given you. Keep telling him you love him until you begin to feel what you are saying. Believe me, he, a thousand miles away, will hear your message.

If you have ill will toward anyone, if you are prejudiced against anyone, if you have accused anyone even in your silent thought of injustice, or if you have criticized anyone, sit down alone at night before retiring and mentally ask him to forgive you. Calling him by name, silently confess to him what you have done and ask his forgiveness, telling him as you do the others, over and over again, that you love him and are sure there is nothing but God's perfect love between you. Never retire until you have thus definitely "cleaned the slate" as regards yourself and every other human being, definitely *for*given—given love "for"—everyone. Keep at this until all the tightened cords that have been cutting off the free flow of God's love and life through you are loosened; until a habit of forgiving is established within you.

This is what Jesus meant by "seventy times seven." This spirit of perfect love and forgiveness will often heal the worst disease by opening the channel for omnipresent love and life to flow through unobstructed.

VII

Power in the Name of
Jesus Christ

"Truly, truly, I say to you, if you ask anything of the Father, he will give it to you in my name." (John 16:23)

That the name of Jesus Christ is a real, practical, wonder-working, result-producing power there is no doubt.

In the Acts of the Apostles we find that, immediately following the death and resurrection of Jesus, Peter and John one day instantly healed *. . . a man lame from birth . . . whom they laid daily at that gate of the temple which is called Beautiful to ask alms . . . .* (Acts 3:2) This healing was done through Peter by the spoken word: *". . . in the name of Jesus Christ of Nazareth, walk."* (Acts 3:6)

We further read that: *. . . immediately his*

feet and ankles were made strong. And leaping up he stood and walked and entered the temple with them, walking and leaping and praising God. And all the people saw him walking and praising God, and recognized him as the one who sat for alms at the Beautiful Gate of the temple; and they were filled with wonder and amazement at what had happened to him. . . .

And when Peter saw it he addressed the people, "Men of Israel, why do you wonder at this, or why do you stare at us, as though by our own power or piety we had made him walk? The God of Abraham and of Isaac and of Jacob, the God of our fathers, glorified his servant Jesus . . . by faith in his name, has made this man strong . . . ." (Acts 3:7-10, 12, 13, 16)

The following day when the rulers of the Jews, the high priests and others, were gathered together, they set Peter and John (whom they had arrested the night before for preaching and healing in this name) in their midst and began to ask: *"By what power, or by what name, did you do this?"* Then Peter, filled with the Holy Spirit, said to them, *"Rulers of the people and elders . . . be it known to you all, and to all the people of Israel, that by the name of Jesus Christ . . . whom God raised from the dead, by him this man is standing before you well. . . . And there is salvation in no one else, for there is no other name under heaven given among men by which we must be saved.''* (Acts 4:7, 8, 10, 12)

Later on in the ministry of Peter we read of his healing Aeneas, who had been in bed eight years, sick of palsy. Paul in the same way healed instantly a woman possessed with a "spirit of divination."

When Isaiah prophesied the coming of the Savior, he said: *"Behold, a young woman shall conceive and bear a son, and shall call his name Immanuel.''* (Isa. 7:14) *Immanuel* means "God with us." The Hebrew name *Jesus* means savior, *Christ* means the anointed of God; Jesus Christ, the Savior anointed of God; Immanuel, God with us.

When the Christ, the Anointed, the very Son of God, came to abide in Jesus, the result was the fullest conscious expression of the invisible Father that had ever occurred; and the very names that contain all power were given to this child by those devout souls who were open enough to receive them by direct illumination of the Spirit.

The name of Jesus Christ holds all power within it.

We know that all sensations, all impressions, either mental or physical, that reach us from without or within reach us through vibrations of one sort or another. We also know that different words spoken produce different effects. If one doubt this, let him speak out into the formless ether the word *power* repeatedly. Then let him by way of experiment take the word *weakness* and do the same for a day; or take the words *love* and *hate,* or any other opposing words, and watch the results. As we ascend from the outer or lower region, the physical, to the higher or more spiritual self living at the center, the vibratory movements by which all information or help is given become finer and subtler but infinitely more powerful.

The name or words *Jesus Christ,* with all their original meaning behind them and embodied in them, produce spiritual vibrations of infinite fineness and power. The master of spiritual things understood this, and many times as He was about to leave His humble disciples and was giving them last instructions He tried to impress upon them the truth that there is power in His name to accomplish things.

"Truly, truly, I say to you, if you ask anything of the Father, he will give it to you in my name. Hitherto you have asked nothing in my name; ask, and you will receive, that your joy may be full." (John 16:23, 24)

Jesus Christ is a revelation of God in us. He is invisible God made visible. Jesus Christ is God-with-us made visible. This is exactly what we all need and desire, did we but know it. This same Christ abiding within you and me is God come forth to center or focus Himself in humanity. *. . .We have this treasure in earthen vessels, to show that the transcendent power belongs to God and not to us.* (II Cor. 4:7)

Because of the intimate relationship we may need to remind ourselves that the greatness of the power is from God, and not from ourselves. Of ourselves we can do nothing. All the power we have comes to us and through us from the Spirit of God.

When a person is given authority to speak or act in the name of a king or of a chief executive, his speaking or acting carries with it the full power vested in the ruler together with that of the entire government behind him. When using the name with full authority, we speak in the name of Jesus Christ, the anointed Son of God, the Savior unto whom has been given all authority, in heaven and on earth, we become even as He is, in this world, and we set in motion a mighty though invisible force to accomplish that whereto our word is sent.

Is your way so hedged in by difficulties that

you do not know which way to turn?

Jesus Christ says, "I am the way." Take His name and use it. There is surely power in it to open ways that the finite mind never dreamed of. Let your silent affirmation constantly be: *Christ is the way now; Christ is the way made visible, for Christ is God-with-us made visible, or the invisible way made visible.*

Let go all external ways and see the marvelous way that will appear before you when you trust this word spoken in His name.

Do all the doors of escape from physical or mental bondage in your daily life seem closed to you?

Jesus Christ says, "I am the door." Stand still and see the salvation that He will work for you when you say: *Christ is the door, the open door made visible this moment. God-with-me is my Savior and deliverer.* Says the Christ within us this very day, right in the midst of our seeming bondage of environment or circumstances, "I have set before thee a door opened, which none can shut." Jesus Christ is the open door. We must first stop all external planning for escape and then enter by faith and by continual affirmation that Christ is now the open door made visible.

Does your life seem dark and gloomy, covered

by a thick, black darkness wherein is no light?

Remembering that Jesus Christ is God-with-us made visible, recall what He said: *"I am the light of the world; he who follows me will not walk in darkness, but will have the light of life."* (John 8:12) It is God speaking to you. Take up the name and remember that whatever you ask in His name, He will do. Your darkness will soon glow with the true *"light which lights every man, coming into the world."*

Does sickness reign in your body?

Still God-with-us made visible is the remedy.

"For as the Father has life in himself, so he has granted the Son also to have life in himself . . . ." (John 5:26)

Is your illness a desperate one?

"I am the resurrection and the life; he who believes in me, though he die, yet shall he live . . . ." (John 11:25) Your case is not quite so bad as "dead," is it? Even if it is, just let go of everything else and take up the all-powerful, all-prevailing name: "Jesus Christ is my life. Christ is God made visible. The life more abundant is this same Christ within me made visible now. He that believeth on this name (the power of the name), though he were dead yet am I his resurrection." *If the Spirit of him who raised Jesus from the dead dwells in you, he who raised*

Christ Jesus from the dead will give life to your mortal bodies also through his Spirit which dwells in you. (Rom. 8:11)

This is the message coming out of the silence from the invisible Father to His children: *". . . ask, and you will receive, that your joy may be full."* (John 16:24) This is a marvelous message indeed!

Christ in us is our all-sufficiency in all things. *Is.* It is a finished condition as far as He is concerned; but we must bring it forth into the material world of manifestation by claiming it (speaking the word of it in His name) and sticking to it through thick and thin no matter what the appearance is.

There is a marvelous power for protection and deliverance in this name when it is simply and earnestly spoken. In times of great mental disturbance or of lack of wisdom, in times when peace and harmony seem to have fled from the home, or when one is in the presence of impure-minded persons or of any false teaching or association, just quietly repeating within one's own heart the sacred and all-powerful name of Jesus Christ will not only keep one's mind in perfect peace but it will radiate marvelous living power from the indwelling divine pesence.

The name of the Lord is a strong tower;
the righteous man runs into it and is safe.

(Prov. 18:10)

Seek often to retire from the world of noise to find revelation of the Christ in your own soul. Sit down quietly and alone and with closed eyes begin to say: *Jesus Christ is now present. He is within me.* Say the words. Say them. You do not need to say anything else, just repeat the name. It will bring wonderful realization of the divine presence. One moment's real conscious communion with the Son of God is of more worth than a thousand worlds.

VIII

Life a Ministry

". . . Whoever would be great among you must be your servant, and whoever would be first among you must be slave of all. For the Son of man also came not to be served but to serve, and to give his life as a ransom for many." (Mark 10:43-45)

Looked at from a purely commercial standpoint, the life of Jesus Christ was a failure. His place in the world was obscure, His occupation a humble one. The work of His hands commanded only the usual recompense. From the world's point of view His contribution was merely that of an average man.

Even after His public life began He seemingly failed just as he had before. He made Himself no reputation among men. Even in the events where

His greatest visible success lay, the delivering of men from sorrow and trouble, He sometimes failed. "He saved others; himself he cannot save," they cried when deriding Him. All the way to His ignominious death He stood before self-satisfied men, chief priests, and Pharisees as a failure. Why? Because He and these men lived from entirely different standpoints. Men lived largely from the external; Jesus lived from within. Men reckoned success then as the world reckons success today, largely in terms of numbers and figures and the possession of external things.

After two thousand years we can see that the life of Jesus Christ, lived so obscurely, so unostentatiously, was not the failure it seemed; that He was living a life that in the long run was the only successful one. For today, when His contemporaries have passed away and are forgotten, His life stands forth as the inspiration of all love and all goodness, the inspiration of all success.

". . . *The Son of man came not to be ministered unto, but to minister*" (Matt. 20:28 A.V.) and all Godlike living is the spirit of ministry unto others. Someone has given the following definitions:

Selfishness: mine, not thine.

Justice: mine and thine.

Love: thine, not mine.

We speak of love as unselfish or selfish. There is no such thing as selfish love. Love gives; selfishness expects to receive. The law of love must be the law of giving, the law of ministration to others, not from sense of duty but from spontaneity and delight. What mother ministers to her children from duty? What father makes daily provision for his children because he is their father and the law says he must? Why, the very heart of parenthood springs out spontaneously and with joy supreme to minister to the child in every possible way even before it can ask or think what it wants.

Pure love always asks, "What can I give?" never "What shall I receive?" God is pure love. Parenthood is a little of God, so to speak, come forth into manifestation, the offspring of God.

God, the source of all life spiritual and physical, God, the only source of real success and joy, abides in Christ within us.

God gives without thought or hope of return. So do we as soon as we become conscious of an indwelling Christ; we cease to expect or desire to be ministered unto.

If we would live the life of real success, real joy, real Christlikeness, we must keep the current turned to flow from within outward instead of in the opposite direction.

God says: *". . . if you pour yourself out for the hungry and satisfy the desire of the afflicted, then shall your light rise in the darkness and your gloom be as the noonday. And the Lord will guide you continually, and satisfy your desire with good things, and make your bones strong; and you shall be like a watered garden, like a spring of water, whose waters fail not."* (Isa. 58:10, 11) Of course if you pour yourself out, it could not be otherwise. All drawing out of the soul is a drawing out directly from the Fountainhead within, from Him who is all life, all light, all good, to minister Him unto others. And as the water of life flows through you to minister to others it must first refresh you with new life, and light, and joy.

Oh, how we have mistaken and misunderstood Him who is the Way! How we have missed the joy of service by letting our ministry to others be from a sense of duty, thus striving to satisfy the conscience, in a way, by afflicting our souls and feeling that such a sacrifice was acceptable to God and in some way an aid to our growth in grace.

"Is not this the fast that I choose: to loose the bonds of wickedness, to undo the thongs of the yoke, to let the oppressed go free, and to break

every yoke? Is it not to share your bread with the hungry, and . . . when you see the naked, to cover him . . .? Then shall your light break forth like the dawn, and your healing shall spring up speedily; your righteousness shall go before you, the glory of the Lord shall be your rear guard. Then you shall call, and the Lord will answer; you shall cry, and he will say, Here I am." (Isa. 58:6-9)

No one can live to himself and not be a failure both spiritually and physically. Such living causes the stream of life and light to form back-water, and the body as well as the soul shrivels for want of new supplies from the Fountainhead. It is only when you draw out your soul that your healing shall spring forth speedily, because health is nothing less than the life more abundant that Christ made manifest through the body. "I am . . . the life," said Jesus Christ. "The life" thus implies His recognition of only one life. God does not live unto Himself. His greatest desire is to get into expression, into visibility, as life, love, joy, all good.

The divine Father of us all is forever trying to manifest Himself in what the Scottish minister, George MacDonald, called "a reckless extravagance of abundance." He might have manifested Himself in a few flowers; but instead He fills to overflowing the very brooksides, the unused and often unseen valleys with a perfect wealth of foliage and beautiful blossoms. He gives from the very joy of giving. What He has given in nature without our interference is truly an "extravagance of abundance." Can this desire to get into expression as the fullness of all that He is— not of all that He has—be less than it is in nature when it comes to His highest creation, humankind? Surely not.

Imagine a great reservoir fed inexhaustibly from ever-living springs within itself. Leading out from this reservoir but never separated from it are innumerable little streams, each ending in a fountain. A fountain is simply a receiving and distributing station, it is never self-existent or self-feeding. Each one of the fountains is an individual center for distributing the water it receives. It is constantly renewed from the one great source without any effort on its own part. Its sole business is to distribute what it receives. At its external extremity each little fountain is separate and distinct from all the others, but at its inner extremity, at the center, it is one with them all.

This is exactly God's relation to His children. He is the reservoir, we are the receiving and distributing stations; He is the vine; we the branches. *One God and Father of us all, who is above all and through all and in all.* (Eph. 4:6)

There is no obstruction between this great reservoir and any individual fountain except what we put there. Each one is, as Emerson says, the inlet, and may become the outlet of all there is in God. But each one must keep his own fountain free for the great stream to flow through. He must not let it get dammed up by selfishness. There must be a constant outflow in order to keep water pure, cold, and invigorating. No one need plead with the water in a spring to flow. It is bound by its very nature and "desire" to make room for the pressure of new waters, which are ever crowding up from its living center to flow wherever they can find a free outlet. If one outlet becomes obstructed the water simply seeks more room through another, for flow it must by the law of its being.

New life, new wisdom, new love and joy and power are waiting to flood our being from the great reservoir, God: *"What no eye has seen, nor ear heard, nor the heart of man conceived, what God has prepared for those who love him."* (I Cor. 2:9)

But if, either consciously or unconsciously, we close up the outlet by refusing to give out to others what we receive, or by mentally living unto ourselves alone, if as a part of worldly wisdom we repress the God-given loving impulse to distribute freely and without thought or hope of return, we so choke up the living stream of good that God is powerless to pour into us the very things for which we may be praying.

Christ is the light of the world. Christ is within us. This light is ever fed from the great fountain of all light, the Father in Him. God made each one of us to be a radiating center, constantly shining outward toward others in a spirit of ministry and giving. If you draw out your soul to satisfy the afflicted, then your light will break forth as the morning and your darkness will be as the noonday (Isa. 58:8-10); *"for I, very Christ, who have come to abide within you, I am the light of the world, and when anyone draws out his soul he draws Me out."*

But if you put a covering over your light by harboring the thought of not letting your neighbor receive from you anything for which he makes no return, you will simply find yourself walking in the darkness. *"If then the light in you is darkness, how great is the darkness!"* (Matt. 6:23) As Christian Gellert said: *Whoever in the darkness lighteth another with this lamp [Christ] lighteth himself also; and the light is not of ourselves, it is of Him who appointeth the suns in their courses.*

The Spirit of Christ is ever the spirit of ministration. We are not called upon to give that which we have not but only that which we have. When Peter and John were going into the Temple and saw a certain lame man lying at the gate of the Temple, where he daily asked alms, Peter said to him, "Look on us." Acts says: . . . *he fixed his attention upon them, expecting to receive something from them. But Peter said, "I have no silver and gold, but I give you what I have; in the name of Jesus Christ of Nazareth, walk."* (Acts 3:5, 6) Who shall say that Peter did not give more than any amount of money or alms? *". . . Give, and it will be given to you; good measure, pressed down, shaken together, running over, will be put into your lap. For the measure you give will be the measure you get back."* (Luke 6:38)

Jesus knew the immutable law when He said this. He knew that *"every good gift and every perfect gift is from above, coming down from the Father of lights."* He also knew that all giving tends to larger receiving.

*One man gives freely, yet grows all the
    richer;*

79

another withholds what he should give,
and only suffers want.

(Prov. 11:24)

Question Helps

Answers to all the following questions can be found in the text.

The terms used in the questions are of course found in the text and are those commonly used in Truth literature. The questions are asked with the object of inducing thought on the part of the student.

When the ideas behind the words in the text are mastered, the student will be able to answer the questions.

Chapter I

Good Tidings of Great Joy

1. What are the "good tidings of great joy which shall be to all the people"?
2. What is the kingdom of heaven?

3. Can others do what Jesus did? Do we have proof of this?

4. What three aims did Jesus have in His teaching and ministry?

5. What is the most important thing that Jesus taught?

6. Is God separate from us and the world?

7. Does God give physical help or does He give spiritual help only?

8. Is hopeless submission to suffering a spiritual grace?

9. Are suffering and hardship productive of spiritual virtue?

10. What should be our attitude toward any "evil" situation in our life?

Chapter II

The Will of God

1. What is God?

2. What is God's will for us?

3. What was the mission of Jesus?

4. If God's will for us is always good, why are not all our prayers answered immediately?

5. Since God supplies our every need, why do we have to pray?

6. Can we change the conditions in our lives that we do not want? How?

7. How can we be certain that it is God's will for us to be happy?

8. How can we avoid or overcome sickness?

9. How must we prepare ourselves to accept God's gifts?

10. Why do good and sincere Christians sometimes have to undergo all sorts of difficulties?

Chapter III

Life More Abundant

1. What is the true nature of life?

2. Can we depend on physical means alone to sustain abundant life in us?

3. Do we get wisdom out of books?

4. Does praise have power?

5. Do our words have power?

6. How many kinds of life are there in the world?

7. Why do we say that man is the highest,

fullest form of God manifested as life?

8. H. Emilie Cady says: "God's gifts are to all alike." If this is true, and God is the source of health, why are some people sick and others well?

9. Why does Unity stress the importance of using only good words?

10. If we are trying to overcome a condition of ill health, is it wrong to seek the help of physicians or other healing agencies?

Chapter IV

Christ in You

1. What is the real nature of man?

2. What is the one substance of the universe?

3. Since Unity does not believe that God is a person, why do we and why did Jesus refer to Him as "our Father"?

4. Is Jesus the Savior of humankind?

5. What is the Christ in you?

6. The Bible tells us that man is created in the image and after the likeness of God. Does this mean that God has arms and legs and a body as

we have?

7. Did God create the world and all that is in it and then cast it adrift?

8. Since man is created in the image of God, he is therefore perfect in essence. Why then is there so much trouble and suffering in the world?

9. What is the new birth that the Bible speaks of?

10. How are we "saved" from our "sins"? What is the Unity teaching about salvation?

Chapter V

Faith

1. What is hope? What is belief? What is faith?

2. What is understanding faith? Blind faith?

3. What are the two principles upon which one can base understanding faith?

4. Can we really receive anything we ask for?

5. If faith is necessary to success in prayer, should a person who does not have faith pray?

6. H. Emilie Cady says that all answer to

prayer depends on faith. How then can a person's prayer be answered if he has no faith?

7. Should we let contrary appearances interfere with our desires?

8. Explain why H. Emilie Cady stresses the importance of believing that we receive now instead of in the future.

9. Is there such a thing as the supernatural? Are there miracles?

10. What part does faith play in spiritual healing? In the demonstration of prosperity?

Chapter VI

Giving and Forgiving

1. Can a person love God as long as he dislikes or hates any other person?

2. Explain why God cannot answer our prayers if we hold ill will or a grudge against someone.

3. Does man have free will?

4. What is the relationship between God and man?

5. Is any sin too great to be forgiven?

6. Describe how you would go about forgiving someone who has done you an injustice.

7. What connection exists between forgiveness and healing?

8. In what three ways do we shut ourselves off from the Christ light?

9. Why is it necessary for us to forgive before we can be forgiven?

10. What is the unpardonable sin?

Chapter VII

Power in the Name of Jesus Christ

1. What is in a name?

2. What is the meaning of the name "Jesus Christ"?

3. Was Jesus more than a man?

4. Is our prayer more effective if we pray in the name of Jesus Christ? Why?

5. Unity teaches that no prayer is ever unanswered. If this is true, why does our prayer sometimes appear to be unanswered?

6. What does it mean to take God's name in vain?

7. What is the power in the name of Jesus Christ?

8. What is meant by "I am the way"?

9. What evidence does the Bible provide that the name of Jesus Christ has power to heal?

10. What is the technique of the silence?

Chapter VIII

Life a Ministry

1. Was Jesus Christ a failure?

2. What is success? What is failure?

3. In this chapter what does H. Emilie Cady mean by "ministry"?

4. Suppose you have no money and none is in sight. What ideas in this chapter would help you to overcome this condition?

5. Name six ways in which we keep our good from coming to us.

6. The Bible says, "*. . . the measure you give will be the measure you get back.*" Does this mean that if we give someone a dollar, someone else will give us a dollar?

7. What kind of gifts should we give?

8. From what standpoint should we make our gifts?

9. From what standpoint does God give to us?

10. If we should stop giving, what would happen to us?

Printed U.S.A.   35-F-8296-5M-12-85